ANXIETY ATTACKS

ANXIETY ATTACKS

by KAREN RANDAU

Rapha Publishing
Houston and Dallas, TX

Anxiety Attacks
by Karen Randau

Second Printing, 1992
ISBN: 0-945276-25-7
Printed in the United States of America

Contents

INTRODUCTION

Anxiety is frequently experienced by people living in today's society. Most people are able to deal with a small amount of anxiety in their lives. But if you are like some people, anxiety can wrap itself tightly around your chest until it feels as if it will suffocate you. People who suffer from feelings like these, called anxiety attacks, frequently attempt to hide the problem, which makes them feel isolated, lonely, and convinced that they are going crazy.

Research by the National Mental Health Institute shows that anxiety disorders affect twenty to thirty million people in the United States. That is ten percent of the population. It is the number one mental-health problem for women. The second largest mental-health problem for men, it falls directly behind alcoholism and drug abuse. This booklet is intended to help you understand the frightening mystery about your anxiety, and to help loosen its suffocating hold on you. In the following pages, you will be challenged to take a fearless look at yourself, your belief systems, and your defense mechanisms. You will discover long-suppressed feelings that may have impeded your ability to live a fulfilling life and develop positive relationships. You will learn basic techniques for living a balanced lifestyle.

Though not a recovery program, this booklet can give you ideas about how you can launch yourself into recovery from debilitating anxiety attacks.

What Is Anxiety?

The beginning of recovery from an anxiety disorder is learning to recognize it in your life. It is helpful to learn the distinction between healthy fears, which protect you, and the out-of-control fears in anxiety and panic attacks, which cause you harm.

Fear is a healthy reaction to impending harm. It is a signal that spells danger and the need for action and is usually accompanied by an adrenalin rush. Situations that justify this kind of fear include:

- Being in a car accident;
- Seeing a child about to touch a hot stove;
- Facing a wild animal ready to attack.

Anxiety is a constant high level of tension over something that may or may not occur. It can be a vague feeling of losing control or that something bad is about to happen. Like fear, healthy anxiety is a warning that tells you something is wrong. Although the Bible says in Matthew 6:25-34 not to worry about your welfare, people tend to feel concerned about things such as the following:

- The bills are due but there is insufficient money to pay them;
- A family member is acting strangely and you do not know how to help.

The roots of unhealthy anxiety are firmly planted in past events. Scenes of the past start playing in your head, and you superimpose past pain over what *might* happen in the future. You may not know exactly what you are afraid of, or that something bad will indeed happen, but you choose to fear anyway. A few symptoms of an anxiety attack include:

- Rapid heartbeat
- Tense muscles
- Nausea
- Dry mouth
- Heat waves
- Chills
- Inability to think clearly
- Feeling detached from yourself
- Fear of going crazy.

Common forms of anxiety include the following:

- Sudden and unexplained uneasiness that subsides within an hour or two;
- Gradually increasing uneasiness about driving, seeing a doctor, confronting someone, etc.;
- Fear that causes consistent avoidance of specific situations;
- Intense worry about something that might happen in a situation usually avoided.

It is normal for anyone occasionally to experience any of these forms of anxiety. They become "anxiety disorders" when they become extremely intense, last months beyond the end of the stressful event, or interfere with normal functioning in your life. Types of anxiety disorders include:

- *Agoraphobia*: fear of being in open spaces, having panic attacks, or being in a place where escape would be difficult;
- *Social phobias*: fear of being embarrassed;
- *Simple phobia*: fear of a specific object or situation;
- *Generalized anxiety disorder*: persistent worry that continues at least six months;
- *Obsessive-compulsive disorder*: recurring yet senseless ideas, thoughts, images, or impulses (obsessions) and the behaviors (compulsions) that are intended to alleviate the anxiety produced by the obsessions.

Panic is fear and anxiety that is out of control. It evokes a compulsion to run from uncomfortable situations. The symptoms are the same as anxiety with several additional signs:

- Sweaty palms
- Ringing ears
- Dizziness
- Choking
- Intense loneliness.

More than three panic attacks a month indicate a "panic disorder" and this disorder requires professional treatment.

What Causes Anxiety Attacks?

Anxiety attacks are a symptom of emotional overload. You are no longer able to recognize and deal with your own feelings. You have learned to deny them either by concealing them or disguising the feelings as something else. These emotions must be brought forth and recognized so they can be put into perspective rather than continue to haunt you.

Who Is Likely to Be Anxious?

Everyone is likely to experience anxiety from time to time. But why are some people more likely to be dominated by the emotions caused by anxiety?

In their book *Worry Free Living* (Thomas Nelson), authors Frank Minirth, Paul Meier, and Don Hawkins submit that "the more insecure we are, the more we strive for attention, fame, and success." It stands to reason that the more insecure you feel and the harder you try to impress others, the more likely you are to suffer from anxiety.

If that is true, why are some people more insecure than others? What causes these people to lose jurisdiction over their confidence and emotions?

As Edmund Bourne suggests, both "nature and nurture" can contribute to anxiety. My research indicates the "nature and nurture equation" consists of heredity, birth order, temperament type, and childhood memories.

Anxiety Genes?

According to Bourne, some people have a genetic predisposition for certain types of anxiety disorders: ". . . it is estimated that 15-25 percent of children growing up with at least one agoraphobic parent become agoraphobic themselves, while the rate of agoraphobia in the general population is only 5 percent." However, how much of this predisposition is inherited and how much is learned?

More convincing is Bourne's suggestion that if one identical twin suffers from some form of anxiety, "the probability of the other identical twin having an anxiety disorder ranges from 31-88 percent, depending on the study you're looking at."

Whether inherited or learned or both, mental health disorders are overcome by employing a balance of recovery methods.

Temperament: The Unique You

A person's temperament is another factor to consider in our look at anxiety-prone people. Your temperament type adds dimension to your emotional reaction to life.

The idea that temperament impacts behavior is not new. Early philosophers theorized about it. Thousands of people throughout history have further shaped the concept. Bourne suggests that some people inherit a personality (temperament) that "predisposes you to be overly anxious."

Many experts describe a "Type A" personality as the most likely to be troubled by anxiety. These are the hard workers who pay extreme attention to every detail, whether in their work, at home, or in personal appearance. They drive themselves to succeed in all they do and have little patience for people who do not share their passion for hard work. They are often seen in responsible leadership positions.

But what if you are an anxiety sufferer and not in the "Type A" group? Does this mean you are abnormal? I used to wonder about that myself because I am not a "pure" Type A. Then I came across an explanation of temperament types that gave me more insight into myself.

Childhood Memories: A Portrait of What's Inside You

Childhood memories reveal the breeding ground where your birth order and temperament type meld to form the adult you become. Your first memories provide an interesting filter for how you think, view life, form relationships, deal with emotions, and shape your self-image.

In their book *Unlocking the Secrets of Your Childhood Memories* (Thomas Nelson), Kevin Leman and Randy Carlson suggest that out of the millions of memories adults accumulate over a lifetime, they recall only those events from childhood that support their present view of themselves and the world around them.

One of my first memories was romping in the yard outside my house with my older sister. She and I were inseparable; we were best pals. We laughed and ran, squealing with delight as only little girls (ages two and four) could. My hair bounced as I chased my sister and then she chased me. I wore only underwear, but I was in my own backyard, so I felt safe, free, and happy.

My bare feet seemed to glide through the grass and a wet spot where soft, slippery mud oozed through my toes. It was wonderful!

Suddenly, my mother's angry face appeared in the window. "You girls get in this house right now and get some clothes on," she yelled as she opened the screen door to let us in.

I immediately felt confined. *I don't want to come into the house,* I thought as I walked up the stairs to the house. *I want to continue running and playing.* But my mother's dreadful expression and voice revealed her anger. I knew my mother would never hurt me, and she never has, yet I was afraid to ever displease her again.

My entire body cooperated in my resentment toward my mother. My face heated up, I thrust out my bottom lip, walked past her into the house, folded my arms in front of me, and plopped down on the floor. *I won't enjoy anything else all day,* I resolved defiantly. (I guess I showed my mother.)

It is not hard to figure out that I like to be free. I love the outdoors. I am also fiercely independent and do not like having people tell me what to do. In fact, each time someone tells me what to do, I feel exactly the way I did when my mother ruined my outdoor romp by telling me to come inside before I was ready.

I also dislike having people angry with me. All it takes is a single look of dissatisfaction to reduce my emotions to those of a two-year-old afraid to anger her mother ever again.

Naturally, my outward reactions rarely reveal my inner unrest. But now that I understand the significance of my first memory, I realize that I have spent much of my life putting effort into being perceived as a "good girl." I am very anxious to please others. I am also a middle child, meaning I often compromise my own needs to earn the acceptance of others. As a melancholic, I judge myself harshly when I fail to be accepted by everyone I meet.

Many people who suffer from anxiety are insecure due to growing up in dysfunctional homes. Some of the problems that plague such families include alcoholism, excessive drug use, emotional and/or physical abuse, and extreme forms of discipline. Young children sense all forms of dysfunction and respond to them in a variety of ways.

Your memories will unveil a lot of information about you. Perhaps your childhood home was not dysfunctional or unhealthy. The source of your anxiety may be difficult to pinpoint. A number of previous incidents may have contributed to your current condition—some which may have seemed insignificant at the time they occurred.

But keep sorting through your memories. They will help you form a mental painting of your life and emotional makeup. And they will help shed light on the root causes of your anxiety.

A word of caution: use the information you discover to understand yourself, and not to make excuses for your anxiety. Your goal should be to *overcome* your anxiety.

How Beliefs Trap Us

Beliefs are the opinions we form of ourselves and life. We arrive at our beliefs through observation, whether at home as children or elsewhere as adults. Many people submit themselves to mistaken beliefs that cause them to doubt the significance of themselves. These beliefs motivate fears of failure, rejection, and punishment. These fears ultimately lead to shame and hopelessness.

These deep-seated feelings are the focus of the anxieties that lead to unhealthy behavior. By learning how these beliefs work in your life, you can learn how to change them. This will help you to behave in a healthy manner and to overcome your anxiety.

Fear of failure arises from a belief that you must meet certain standards to feel good about yourself. This belief prompts a tendency toward perfectionism and seeking success. Manipulation and risk avoidance are common with people who have this fear. Romans 3:1 indicates that you are pleasing to God because of your relationship with Jesus. No earthly standards compare to God's love.

Fear of rejection occurs because of a belief that you must gain the approval of others to feel good about yourself. This belief motivates people to unreasonable extremes to please others and over-sensitivity to criticism. Many people avoid the risk of rejection by withdrawing from others. Colossians 1:21-22 says that you are acceptable to God because Jesus paid the price for your sins on the cross. Some of your *behavior* may need to be adjusted, but *you as a person are acceptable to God.* It doesn't matter if other people cannot reach the same level of perfect forgiveness and acceptance. After all, they are only human also. All humans make mistakes.

Fear of punishment extends from the belief that those who fail are unworthy of love and deserve to be punished. This belief inspires a wealth of blaming techniques, including harshly punishing others for your own failures. Withdrawal from God is typical for those who fear punishment. Romans 3:23 says that we all sin—it is our nature. John 4:9-11 says that Jesus satisfied God's wrath for our sins on the cross.

If you have not accepted Jesus as your savior, do so now. Confess to God that you are a sinner and want forgiveness. Thank Jesus, the son of God, for the price He paid to save you from Hell. Invite Jesus to be in control of your life. In your mind, bundle up all the ugliness and shame in your life and hand it to Jesus. Leave it with Him, never retrieving it again. Rest assured that you have no need to fear punishment.

Shame is a feeling caused by the belief that you are "worthless" or unlovable. It is a belief that God has abandoned you because of some sin you have committed. This feeling comes about when people are not taught to esteem themselves as worthwhile, lovable children of God. Because we are limited humans, we do sin, but the chief tenet of Christianity is that God loves you. As a Christian, you are forgiven of your sins. You may not have *accepted* God's forgiveness and the forgiveness of others, even though it has been offered. Perhaps you have not yet sincerely *asked* the forgiveness of God or others. You even may need to forgive *yourself* for being less than perfect. Learning forgiveness as God teaches will help you begin to see yourself as a beloved child of God.

Hopelessness is caused by a mistaken belief that "I am what I am; I cannot change; I am hopeless." Shame, despair, and hopelessness are the fruits of this belief. It produces passivity, loss of creativity, and isolation. John 3:3-6 says you are a new creation in Christ. This is the rebirth we experience when we accept Jesus as our savior. You are a new, beautiful, fresh *flower* in Christ, perfect and unstained. Ask God to change you, and He will. But it is important to not forget to obey when He tells you how to achieve change through Him. You get these messages through prayer and Scripture reading.

Thoughts: How You Communicate With Yourself

Your beliefs strongly prejudice your thoughts. Thoughts about ourselves are often referred to as "self-talk." This aptly describes the idea that thinking is how we talk to ourselves.

Experts agree that "what-if" self-talk has a negative impact on your emotional health. Because this kind of thinking can become as automatic as driving a car, you may not be aware that you torture yourself this way. Negative thoughts are self-defeating and produce equally self-defeating behavior. Recognizing and learning to change these negative thoughts is imperative to your recovery, but it is a process that takes time. It is not easy to overcome the misdirected thinking that has been guiding you your whole life. Reading Scripture is a good tool that helps realign your thoughts with God's.

The Scriptures are full of encouragement for Christians to carefully manage their thoughts and lead peaceful lives. Romans 5:1 and Colossians 1:20 offer assurance of peace with God through His son Jesus Christ. In John 14:27, Jesus offers a peace different than the world offers and says not to worry or be afraid. Isaiah 26:3 promises peace to those whose minds are fixed on God, and Ephesians 2:14 says that Jesus *is* your peace.

The next time you are tempted to be afraid, consider that in Romans 8:28 God promises to work everything out for your good, that Philippians 4:19 assures that God will supply your needs, and that Philippians 4:13 promises that He will equip you to do whatever is required.

DEFENSE MECHANISMS

Defense mechanisms develop through the need for survival. For example, when we are threatened with a physical blow, we throw up our hands to ward it off. When threatened with other types of blows, such as verbal attacks or emotional trauma, we use defenses to withstand the attack. Seen in this way, it is clear that defenses are necessary for us to survive when we are threatened. Sometimes, however, we get so used to operating from a defensive position, due to frequent abuse or threat of abuse, that we are no longer able to act any way other than defensively. We throw up the defense even when there is no threat.

This is when defense mechanisms become troublesome, inappropriate behaviors based on habit (caused by trauma) that, instead of helping us to survive, interfere with our ability to fully live. What are some of the defense mechanisms you use to deal with difficult situations? The following are some common ones.

Denial: A Game of Hide and Seek

Denying that anxiety has rendered your life out of control is a common defense mechanism. Hiding from problems will not make them go away—in fact, attempts to hide tend to make the problems seem worse than they really are. You are often the only person fooled by your denial mechanism.

Looking for Love

Love is a basic human need. But too many people try to use love to avoid honestly looking at themselves. It becomes another defense mechanism as they jump from one relationship to another, looking for the kind of excitement that eventually died in the last one. You may become a puppet to another person, acting the way they want you to, saying exactly what you think they want to hear. This desperate behavior causes you to lose yourself—and probably resent the object of your affection. All the while, you feel inadequate, maybe even unlovable. You wonder what is wrong with you, why you cannot stay in love, why people do not stay in love with you.

The answer is in Matthew 22:37-39, where Jesus gave us two commandments relating to love. First, we are to love God with all our hearts, souls, and minds. Second, we are to love our neighbors as we would ourselves. An intimate relationship with our Lord Jesus Christ taps us into the only kind of love that can make human relationships work. We must be at peace with God before we can have peace with others. Through our relationships with God, we receive (and learn how to give) unconditional love, the kind of love that forms lasting relationships with other people.

One important factor to consider in relationships is your own sabotage. When we feel unlovable, we tend to go about proving we are right. What ways do you use to sabotage your relationships? Perfectionism? A sharp tongue? Heaping guilt upon yourself and others? Judging others—possibly self-righteously scolding them for imperfections that you also possess? Racing from one unfulfilled relationship to another?

These are all defense mechanisms. They are intended to avoid the hurt of rejection by appearing as if you were the one who rejected. It allows you to feel justified in blaming the other person for the failed relationship. Thus you sink further into the morass of self-pity and self-flagellation, tightening the anxiety-causing strings that control your life which become a noose you place around your own neck.

Life in the Fast Lane

Some people run from themselves by always being busy, never taking time to reflect upon their own feelings. However, you cannot hide under a mountain of activity forever. You will eventually catch up with yourself. Take a moment from your job, committees, and social life for introspection.

Remember that Matthew 22:36 says to love God with all your heart, soul, and mind. When God leads you to serve Him, do it. But sometimes it is best to quietly wait upon the Lord to reveal the areas of your life that keep you from receiving God's total blessing. These blessings often mean arousing and feeling the prickle of numbed emotions; emotions you attempted to hide in the deep corners of your being.

Drowning Your Sorrows

Many people avoid their feelings through drugs and alcohol. This is a course headed for self-destruction, a deliberate act of physical and spiritual suicide. The harm done to us through drugs and alcohol is clearly documented. The fact that a person uses drugs or alcohol in spite of these known dangers so they can numb their own feelings shows that person's desperation to end their pain.

Eating Disorders

Many people run straight to the refrigerator each time something upsets them. It is better to face and deal with emotions rather than destroy your body and self-esteem by overeating.

Other forms of eating disorders include anorexia and bulimia. Anorexics refuse to eat. Bulimics binge and then purge. Both put strain on body functions—and will eventually result in death. They are both slow, torturous suicide. Psychiatric treatment is required to overcome these disorders.

If you can identify with any of these types of defense mechanisms, you need to recognize two things. First, that these defenses can be serious disorders in themselves; they may require treatment of some sort if the disorder has become severe enough. And second, that these are all symptoms of some deeper trouble that stems from your not being able to face some trauma in your life. The key to dealing with trauma is learning to identify, admit, and express your feelings. The following section discusses feelings.

WHAT IS A FEELING?

The bumps of life may convince you that it is safer to withdraw emotionally to avoid negative emotions. But feelings are a packaged deal. Emotional withdrawal eliminates positive as well as negative emotions. For you to identify the problems that cause your anxiety, you must continually read your emotional barometer. You cannot do that by hiding from your feelings. Your anxiety support group can help trigger the process of making friends with your emotions. Group meetings are a safe place to be completely honest about your feelings. This will help you unpack them from the airtight bag into which you have stuffed them. The group also can help you learn how to use your feelings constructively.

What Causes Suppressed Feelings?

Feelings get suppressed in happy homes as often as in unhappy ones. Receiving the message that your feelings are wrong instills a belief that they do not matter. You dismiss them, eventually becoming unable to identify them. The discomfort brought on by not knowing what you are feeling causes anxiety. Symptoms of suppressed feelings include:

- Unexplained or uncontrollable anger;
- Anxiety;
- Depression;
- Psychomatic illness;
- Muscle tension
- Feeling trapped or out of control.

Emotions and Decisions: A Balancing Act

Be careful. Emotions can lead you into situations where your head warns against going. Healthy decisions are made by gathering the facts, discerning what data applies to your situation, and then asking the counsel of other people and God. The final decision must always be based on whether or not your actions will glorify God. That is your obligation, not the glorification of yourself to impress others. Once you have completed the above steps and made a responsible decision, take action. Step out in confidence that God is in control—release yourself from the anxiety about whether or not you made the right decision. Hand it to God.

Learning Healthy Ways to Express Emotion

There are many ways to learn to express your emotions. Keeping a diary is one way that can help you get in touch with your feelings. Watch your own behavior. Note the physical sensations attached to certain behaviors. Attach emotion words to the behavior and physical sensations. Beware of expressing beliefs as emotions ("I feel my boss dislikes me"). Beliefs come from the head ("my boss dislikes me"). Feelings come from the heart ("his unjust treatment makes me feel unliked").

Feelings can be described in both negative and positive words. Positive feeling words include amused, accepted, content, happy, relaxed, and worthwhile. Negative feeling words include afraid, angry, ashamed, desperate, guilty, hurt, insecure, lonely, pressured, stupid, unfulfilled, and worried.

Go back to the previous paragraph and read the feeling words aloud. Use various intonations and observe the sensations the words induce. This is another method of learning to identify feelings.

Many anxiety sufferers fear going crazy if they allow themselves to feel. Fear not. You cannot cause yourself to go crazy. It is true that sometimes feelings are overwhelming. A support group can be helpful. When an emotion peeps its head up from under the rubble you have piled on top of it for all these years, do not run from it. *Feel* it!

If you are numb from years of not allowing yourself to feel, another technique is to think about how someone else might feel if they were behaving the way you are. When you are imagining what others might feel, assume ownership for the fact that *you* imagined that thought. Maybe that is really how *you* feel.

What To Do If Things Get Scary

You can retrain yourself to feel automatically—and without fear. But take it slowly, being careful to nurture yourself each step along the way. Once you take the lid off your feelings, expect a torrent of emotions. You may tap into old rage. If so, discuss healthy ways to express rage in your support group. You may find that you are suddenly crying more. That is okay. You are feeling the fullness of being you. If your emotions begin to get scary, take a time out. You might:

- Practice deep breathing exercises;
- Call a friend;
- Listen to relaxing music;
- Pray;
- Hug your pillow.

Do whatever works for you. If you are prone to panic, plan how you will get yourself through the panic before it happens.

Keep feeling and expressing. Once you get through the initial stages, the uncontrollable tears will subside. If not, seek help from your support group—or find a professional counselor. By all means, do not lock yourself back into a closet of unexpressed emotions.

Learning to Like Yourself

A second aspect of getting in touch with your emotions is learning to like yourself, in spite of the emotions you harbor. Liking yourself comes from inner peace. This kind of peace comes from your relationship with Jesus Christ, not through performance-based relationships, fancy cars, or a high-paying job. Peace is an antidote for loneliness and anxiety. When you become comfortable with yourself, many of the reasons for your anxiety will disappear. That is not to say you will never again feel anxious after you learn to like yourself. However, the intensity of your anxiety attacks and your methods of dealing with your fear will change.

Characteristics of a Peaceful Person

Peaceful people look for ways to be calm, not cause strife. Peaceful people accept that all things work together for those who love God (Romans 8:28). They exude confidence that God will supply their every need (Philippians 4:10-13), and they realize that *needs* are not equal to *wants* (Proverbs 30:7-9). The strength of a peaceful person comes from knowing that the power of Jesus is sufficient to do whatever is required

(Philippians 4:13). They claim the promise of Psalm 29:11: "The Lord will bless His people with peace." We are drawn to peaceful people. Peaceful people have what we want. We avoid restless, anxious people. We already have what they have, and we do not like it.

The Power of Prayer and Meditation

Prayer and meditation on the Scriptures fortifies your self-image, builds your faith, and strengthens your intimacy with God. Time alone with the Lord is the most profitable time of the day. Through the Scriptures you learn that you are perfectly pleasing to God, no matter what worldly standards you fail. The moment you accept Jesus as your savior, you become reconciled with God, and this renders the opinion of others powerless. No sin is so great that Jesus did not already pay for it. You can let go of your anxiety, turning it over to Jesus through prayer and meditation.

Many people do not find peace through their relationship with God because of their image of Him. You can convince yourself that God is harsh and punishing. Or you can accept that He loves you and wants to give you peace. You can begin to look at your circumstances as a learning ground and an opportunity for growth. Or you can be angry at God and continue to live in anxiety. It is your choice. But remember, a person with no peace criticizes, is quick to anger, and displays a negative outlook on life. This kind of person repels people who have a positive outlook.

So if you want to form healthy relationships, you need to be able to attract healthy people. That means *being* healthy so that you can display a peaceful demeanor. After you learn to love yourself, then you can love others in the same unconditional way.

Strengthen Your Strengths

The Bible tells us that success is not measured by what we have or what others think of us. Rather, it is measured by what we do with what we have (Matthew 25:21). Our strengths and weaknesses are what we have. What are your strengths? Exercise them. You may be surprised to find that many of your weaknesses are really strengths—if you use them constructively. In this way, you build your life on a foundation of truth, as the Bible tells you to do in Matthew 7:24-27.

You will fail. We all do. But failure is a stepping stone to success, not an indictment that you are a failure. Just keep strengthening your strengths. As you learn to love and accept yourself for who you are, your anxiety will begin to fade.

Developing Positive Relationships

During an anxiety attack, it helps to call a trusted friend. You need someone who will quietly listen to your reasons for being upset, and then lovingly talk you down off the ceiling. But to have a friend, you must first be one. Healthy friendships improve your physical, emotional, and spiritual life. Unhealthy alliances detract from your life and are not worth the toll they take.

Good friends:

- Accept one another as they are;
- Listen to each other;
- Encourage one other;
- Talk out their problems.

Anything less is not a healthy friendship, and it will tear you down rather than build you up.

Identifying Unhealthy Relationships

Sometimes it is necessary to make a list of the people with whom you have an unhealthy relationship. If both parties are willing to work to improve the relationship, it is best to do so. You never realize the value of a friendship until it fails. However, if a particular relationship continues to harm you, no matter how hard you try to correct the situation, it may be best to end the relationship.

You may know that a relationship is harmful to physical or emotional health but cannot end it. You may be dependent upon that person. Your support group might be able to offer ideas about how to end the relationship. Depending upon the severity of the dependence, you may need to seek professional help.

How to Form Healthy Friendships

Friendships require time and energy. They stand the test of conflict, envy, and hurt feelings. Though intimacy is not the reason for the friendship, intimacy often becomes the byproduct. Following are some suggestions to forming friendships of this type.

- Take a fearless look at your family and past relationships, examining both the good and bad.
- Risk communicating your needs and desires to others, maybe even discussing your conclusions about past relationships with someone else. Do not push for intimacy, but let it happen naturally. Do not avoid closeness out of fear of rejection.
- Learn to communicate openly and honestly, and look for friends that display the willingness and ability to communicate in the same way.
- Know and respect your boundaries and the boundaries of others.

- Pray that God will bring people your way who are emotionally healthy—then accept them as they are.

If your social circle is limited, your support group, church, or other community organization may be a good place to find compatible friends.

Biblical Counsel About Friendships

The book of Proverbs is full of good advice about forming healthy relationships. Proverbs 27:6 says, "Faithful are the wounds of a friend, but the kisses of an enemy are deceitful." When looking for healthy friendships, do not accept empty flattery. Look for someone you can trust to be loyal and honest, someone who can lovingly tell you when you have messed up. This kind of friend helps keep you on track. This is not to say that you should find someone who constantly criticizes. Critical people are insecure and want to prove that you are on their level. Good friends are people who are content with themselves. People who are content with themselves are happy to allow others to be content with themselves. They are not always trying to change others to meet their own standards.

Walking in the love of Jesus brings you into the kind of love that will make your relationships work. Start looking for friends by looking first to God, being ever-mindful that God works through others for your development. Your confidence in your relationship with Jesus determines how well you cope with rejection from other people.

The Role of Prayer in Finding Fulfillment

Philippians 1:3-11 provides an example of loving prayers between friends. Paul prays that his friends will receive love, spiritual knowledge and enlightenment, and the fruits of the Spirit. The Lord's Prayer (Matthew 6:9-13) teaches that prayer consists of:

- Praising God for who He is and what He has done;

- Agreeing with—and submitting to—God's perfect will in your life;
- Asking for your *needs* and the needs of others;
- Confessing sins, asking forgiveness, accepting that forgiveness, and forgiving others;
- Renewal, or continually seeking God for resistance from temptation;
- A closing that reveres God.

To determine the effectiveness of your prayer life, consider the following: Do you *believe* that God will deliver you from your anxiety attacks? Or are your prayers simply spoken as proof to yourself that you tried to calm yourself down? Do you accept God's answers to your prayers, even when He responds in ways other than what you wanted or expected? Remember, He is the one in control, not you. Therefore, He is the one most qualified to decide how to answer your prayers.

In an attempt to be perfect—a perfect employee, a perfect spouse, a perfect parent, a perfect friend, a perfect Christian—do you become more anxiety-ridden than ever before?

Do not allow other people to demand perfection of you. And by all means, do not place that burden on yourself. Finally, do not try to control and manipulate God by trying to specify how He should answer your prayers. For example, instead of saying, "Bring a big, handsome man into my life," it would be more appropriate to simply pray, "Help me find a friend."

The Bible says in John 4:13 that Jesus is your cup of living water. Jesus will provide all your needs—and even be your best friend. Through Him, you can have peace, joy, and love. These are the traits that help you like yourself and form healthy human friendships.

Living a Balanced Lifestyle

A balanced lifestyle is key to experiencing the peace and joy that alleviate anxiety. This includes healthy thinking, proper breathing, food nutrition, exercise, sleep, play, and quiet time with God. It includes friends that share common attitudes with you. And it includes forgiveness and reevaluation of yourself—based on God's direction.

Healthy Thinking

Part of learning to relax is to learning let go of the past. Realize that what is happened has happened. You cannot change the past. All you can do is go on from here. Whether you were abused as a child, betrayed by a trusted friend, or seriously injured in an auto accident, it does no good to hang onto past grief. Choosing to do so is a decision to let anxiety reign in your life. You have learned to let go when you no longer try to control and manipulate people and situations. Constantly attempting to control others causes anxiety.

Another aspect of relaxed thinking is admitting, understanding, and respecting your fears. If you are afraid of spiders, admit it. If driving across town frightens you, be honest about that, too.

When caught up in an anxiety attack, it may be difficult to think clearly. But that is exactly what you need to do. Decide if the fear is well-founded or if it is something you invented. If evidence suggests fear is warranted, take action. If no evidence exists, examine what is going on and determine the *real* cause of the anxiety. For example, you may feel neglected by your spouse or family.

You begin to fear they will reject you, so you distance yourself from them by criticizing and attempting to control them. Your behavior is intended to manipulate your family into paying more attention to you. It has the opposite effect.

A healthier approach is to tell your family that you are feeling neglected and that it makes you afraid they are going to reject you.

It is important not to allow your anxiety to send you blowing in the wind. Rather than quitting your job because you might get fired, discuss your performance with your boss. Instead of cutting all your hair off because you have nothing better to do, examine the reason for your need of attention. Before you eat that eighteenth chocolate chip cookie, think about what void you are trying to fill— and what better ways you could choose to fill it. Ask God for direction.

Plan Ahead

If anxiety makes thinking difficult, panic compounds the confusion. Plan how you will get yourself through your next panic attack. Make a list in preparation for it. Your Panic Plan might remind you to:

- Practice proper breathing;
- Call a friend (phone number);
- If that friend does not answer, call someone else (phone number).
- Read your favorite passage in the Bible (what page is it on in *your* Bible?);
- Pray;
- Skip rope;
- Eat 10 crackers (count them);
- Listen to your favorite song eight times;
- Write down ten ways to make this the best year of your life;
- Go to a quiet place to be alone temporarily (prepare one now).

Remember that you are not going crazy. Believe that your feelings will not harm you. Understand that you will eventually get through it. Do not pump up your fear by running; rather, accept the feeling of panic as something that is part of you. Use the breathing exercises described below to help ease you through it. Above all, stick to your Panic Plan.

Staying Fit

Stretching and exercising your muscles as you breathe helps calm you. The better your physical health, the better you are able to withstand anxiety. Perhaps you could try aerobic activities such as walking, jogging, swimming, and bicycling. These offer both enjoyment and improved fitness—even for former champion couch potatoes.

You know if you are out of shape. You are a champion couch potato if walking up a flight of stairs leaves you gasping for air, strolling around the block renders you unable to get out of bed the next day, or you seem to live in a state of tiredness, lethargy, or boredom. These symptoms may also indicate other health problems so consult your physician before beginning any exercise program. Whatever activity you choose to get back into shape, make it fun.

A good exercise program includes five minutes of stretching, five minutes of slow warm-up activity, ten to thirty minutes of faster aerobic activity, and five minutes of slower cool-down activity. To maintain your motivation, keep a record of your progress. Set goals for yourself and reward yourself for meeting each goal. This is a great way to take care of yourself.

You Are What You Consume

Take an appraisal of your eating habits. Identify the items in your diet which may be contributing to your anxiety. For example, stimulants (such as caffeine and nicotine) do exactly what their name implies. They stimulate you, aggravate anxiety, and trigger panic. Salt, preservatives, and sugar are other substances that can stress your body. Certain foods also may induce allergic reactions such as anxiety, moodiness, insomnia, headaches, and confusion.

Enjoying Life

Anxiety sufferers tend to take life seriously. A very good thing you can do for yourself is to learn to play. Even cleaning house and washing cars can be fun if you let them be. Make a list of activities you enjoy, then make a point of doing them on a regular basis.

For most people, music is a powerful element in enjoying life. Keep a library of soothing music that can help relax you. Memorize the words to hymns that contain a relaxing message for you. Try singing them to yourself when anxiety or panic seizes you.

Wait on the Lord

Remember to depend upon Jesus as your comfort. Be patient. As Hosea 6:3 says, "As surely as the sun rises, He will appear; He will come to us like the winter rains, like the spring rains that water the earth." You are worthy of the loving peace that God provides. When He offers that peace, acknowledge and accept it. As you wait on the Lord, imagine yourself in a peaceful place, the kind of place that brings you pleasure, the kind of place where you would most like to meet the Lord. You do not have to "see" this place, just imagine it.

Experiencing Peace and Joy

We all experience some form of anxiety from time to time. But you can choose how these attacks will affect you. The tips that have been described are ways to deal with your anxiety, so that you can obtain the peace and joy that await you.

TREATMENT OPTIONS

Treatment options consist mainly of group therapy, outpatient counseling, and inpatient treatment.

Support Groups

Groups provide a nonrestrictive atmosphere and a safe environment where you can talk about your anxiety with others who struggle with the same kinds of problems. Led by trained therapists or peers, group participants relate their experiences and offer love and support to one another. Meetings provide a structured way to examine and correct what is wrong.

Not all meetings are alike. Look for the one that best suits your needs—and then stick with it. It may hurt at times, but you must get through the pain before you can find the peace.

Group therapy works for many. Others need more structured settings.

Outpatient Counseling

In outpatient counseling you meet individually with a trained therapist. The private setting makes many people more comfortable than group meetings, though it does not offer the advantage of comparing stories, and solutions with other anxiety sufferers who can assure you that you are not alone and that your condition is treatable. Many people combine outpatient counseling with group meetings.

Although outpatient counseling is generally more costly than self-help groups (which are usually free), many clinics offer a variable fee schedule.

Inpatient Treatment

Inpatient treatment offers a safe setting for dealing with your anxiety issues on an intensive level. Programs vary in duration and techniques. Carefully select an inpatient program that best meets your needs. Your local telephone book may list various centers. Call all of them, asking specific questions about their treatment and philosophies.

Reputable centers offer education, individual therapy, group therapy, and family therapy to help patients understand and modify their lives. Other treatment sometimes includes therapies such as psychodrama, art, music, and recreation.

Spirituality is an important aspect of any treatment program. When searching for a group, counselor, or inpatient setting that is right for you, ask questions about their meaning of the word *spiritual*. If Christian is what you want, request a Christ-centered program. Spiritual does not always equal Christian.

Rapha is the nation's largest manager of of psychiatric and substance abuse treatment from a Christian perspective. Their programs address mental, physical, and spiritual needs to help clients learn how to deal with life by not basing their self-worth on their performance or the opinions of others. For more information on Rapha programs, write 8876 Gulf Freeway, Suite 340, Houston, TX, 77017, or call 1-800-383-HOPE.

The Use of Medications in Treatment of Anxiety

In both outpatient counseling and in-hospital treatment programs, psychiatrists may treat severe cases of anxiety with medication. Be aware that the use of medication should always accompany counseling to help you uncover and deal with the underlying issues that cause your anxiety. Without counseling, the use of medications is merely pulling a veil over your emotions—your problems will not go away. The use of some drugs without counseling can only intensify the situation.

The types of drugs most commonly used for anxiety are tranquilizers. It is your responsibility to understand the side effects of any drugs prescribed to you. Consult your doctor or a library. Tranquilizers can be addictive and should be used for short periods of time. They are required *only* if your anxiety is disabling.

Antidepressants also are used to combat anxiety. These generally are nonaddictive and are most commonly used for people who experience panic with their anxiety attacks.

Editor's note:

At Rapha, we believe that small groups can provide a nurturing and powerful environment to help people deal with real-life problems such as depression, grief, fear, eating disorders, chemical dependency, codependency and all kinds of other relational and emotional difficulties. The warmth, honesty and understanding in those groups helps us understand why we feel and act the way we do. And with the encouragement of others, we can take definitive steps toward healing and health for ourselves and our relationships.

Not all groups, however, provide this kind of "greenhouse" for growth. Some only perpetuate the guilt and loneliness by giving quick and superficial solutions to the deep and often complex problems in our lives.

We urge you to find a group of people in your church, or in a church near you, where the members provide acceptance, love, honesty and encouragement. Rapha has many different books, workbooks, leader's guides and types of training so that people in these groups can be nurtured in the love and grace of God and focused on sound biblical principles to help them experience healing and growth. Rapha offers small-group materials and training for a wide variety of needs, including: self-esteem issues, depression, chemical dependency, codependency, eating disorders, and other emotional and relational problems.

To obtain a free list of the materials we have available, please write to us at:

Rapha, Inc.
8876 Gulf Freeway, Suite 340
Houston, TX 77017

About the Author...

Karen L. Randau is an adult child of an alcoholic with experience as a lay counselor in a Christian mental health facility. She understands the anguish of anxiety from first-hand experience. Her career as an author began at an early age—as soon as she learned to read. Now, as then, her writings represent a time to journal the feelings and desires common to most of us.